THE HISTORY OF NAVIES AROUND THE WORLD

THE HISTORY OF
NAVIES
AROUND THE WORLD

EDITED BY SHALINI SAXENA
SUPPLEMENTAL MATERIAL BY RICHARD BARRINGTON

Britannica®
Educational Publishing

IN ASSOCIATION WITH

ROSEN
EDUCATIONAL SERVICES

Published in 2014 by Britannica Educational Publishing (a trademark of Encyclopædia Britannica, Inc.) in association with The Rosen Publishing Group, Inc.
29 East 21st Street, New York, NY 10010

Distributed exclusively by Rosen Publishing.
To see additional Britannica Educational Publishing titles, go to rosenpublishing.com

First Edition

Britannica Educational Publishing
J.E. Luebering: Director, Core Reference Group
Anthony L. Green: Editor, Compton's by Britannica

Rosen Publishing
Hope Lourie Killcoyne: Executive Editor
Shalini Saxena: Editor
Nelson Sá: Art Director
Brian Garvey: Designer
Cindy Reiman: Photography Manager
Introduction and supplemental material by Richard Barrington

Cataloging-in-Publication Data

The history of navies around the world/editor, Shalini Saxena; supplementary material by Richard Barrington. — First edition.
    pages cm. — (The world's armed forces)
Includes bibliographical references and index.
ISBN 978-1-62275-142-6 (library binding)
1. Navies—History. 2. Naval history. I. Saxena, Shalini, 1982– II. Barrington, Richard, 1961–
V27.H57 2014
359.009—dc23

2013032956

Manufactured in the United States of America

CONTENTS

British naval hero Horatio Nelson. Admiral Nelson won a number of important victories during his time with the Royal Navy. *DEA/G. Nimatallah/De Agostini/Getty Images*

Admiral Horatio Nelson and other great naval commanders of the past might have trouble recognizing today's navies. It's not just the technology that has changed; the role and tactics of today's navies are also vastly different than they were throughout much of naval history, and increasingly the individuals who comprise those navies are also changing.

The technological changes have led to large vessels capable of moving at great speeds, both on and below the surface of the water. Landing craft are designed to move seamlessly from water to dry land, while sophisticated weapons systems combine immense firepower with state-of-the-art radar systems to target enemies on land, on or under the water, or in the air. Meanwhile, satellite positioning systems have made possible navigation with pinpoint precision.

Technology and weapons systems have contributed to the evolution of naval tactics, but so has the nature of modern warfare. On one level, the ability to launch ballistic missiles from ships and submarines makes a navy a valuable part of the nuclear deterrent wielded by global powers. On another level, navies have had to become more agile and versatile. Fighting terrorism and intervening in civil conflicts require the ability to strike swiftly at targets that are often isolated and highly specific. Modern navies have responded to this need with small, high-speed boats and elite fighting units trained for action at sea or on land. In short, as the scope of warfare has become both more global and more localized, navies have had to adapt to both needs.

Even the human face of the navy has evolved over the centuries and can be expected to continue changing in the years ahead. Starting in the second half of the 20th century, some countries around the world began relaxing their policies toward gays and women, allowing gays to serve openly in the military and women to have more prominent roles, including serving in combat. In the 21st century, the United States Navy—the world's largest—followed suit, adopting policies more accepting of gays in the military and women in combat than in the past.

While the image of a sailor has become increasingly more difficult to pin down, so, too, has the definition of a modern navy. Of course, the core of a navy remains ships and sailors, but today's navies also consist of planes and helicopters, commando units, and remote-control vehicles.

This volume will trace the evolution that has led from oar-driven galley ships to nuclear-powered submarines and beyond. Its pages will chronicle some 5,000 years of naval history, and show how new exploits are continuing to add to naval tradition. In describing the navies of today, this book will profile some prominent national navies from around the world, demonstrating how the challenge of mastering the seas is one that inspires people from a variety of cultures.

Ultimately, naval tradition is not just long-lived but is truly a global phenomenon. Understanding that tradition is both a key to understanding history and a clue to the future.

WHAT IS A NAVY?

CHAPTER 1

A navy is the seagoing arm of a nation's military forces. In an army, the individual soldier is the fighting unit. In a navy, however, it is the individual ship that makes up a fighting unit. All members of the crew, from the captain on the bridge to the boiler technician, work together in order to make the ship an effective instrument of combat.

WHY IS A NAVY IMPORTANT?

On April 2, 1982, the military forces of Argentina seized the Falkland Islands, a British possession in the South Atlantic. Three days later a huge task force of Great Britain's Royal Navy sailed from Portsmouth, England, on a mission to recover the islands. Before the end of April the task force had covered the 8,000 miles (13,000 kilometers) between England and the Falklands. Military operations officially began on April 25. Less than 11 weeks later the war was over, and Britain had achieved its goal. Success was made possible by Britain's ability to gain and keep control of the seas, fend off air and sea attacks from Argentina, and put combat units ashore.

"In all history," said Viscount Bernard Law Montgomery, "the nation which has had control of the seas has, in the end, prevailed." This conviction reaffirms a point of view developed by the American naval officer Alfred T. Mahan in 1890. His book, *The Influence of Sea Power upon History, 1660–1783*, is a survey of British naval power. In it he states that a nation needs a strong industrial base and a powerful navy in order to achieve military supremacy and to extend its commerce around the world. The book was one of the most influential military studies and had a very strong influence on the naval buildup in Europe prior to World War I.

For nearly four centuries Great Britain's Royal Navy commanded the sea lanes of the world. During that time Britain lost only one major conflict: the American Revolution. The reason for the loss can in great measure be blamed on inadequate naval power in the face of an alliance of the young United States with France and Spain.

American naval officer and historian Alfred T. Mahan. Mahan's book influenced naval strategy both in the United States and in Europe prior to World War I. *Buyenlarge/Archive Photos/Getty Images*

Command of the seas was a primary ingredient in the Greek defeat of the Persians in the 5th century BCE; in Rome's defeat of Carthage in the 3rd century BCE; in Britain's defeat of France during the Napoleonic Wars; and in the victory of the Allies over Germany, Italy, and Japan in World War II.

COMMAND STRUCTURE

The command structure of modern navies evolved slowly over the centuries. Such early navies as those of Greece and Rome were rather simply run. Ships were guided by an expert seaman and powered by banks of rowers. There was normally a contingent of marines kept in reserve for hand-to-hand combat when an enemy ship was boarded. As naval warfare became more complex, onboard responsibilities were divided among officers and seamen of various ranks. The enormous technological complexities of modern warfare served to create many highly specialized functions. The command structure covered here is that of the United States Navy. Other major navies of the world are similar, though officer titles may vary from country to country.

Naval personnel are ranked in two categories: enlisted men and commissioned officers. There are nine rates (ranks or positions) of enlisted men. The lowest rate is seaman recruit. Above the recruit are seaman apprentice and seaman. The rate of seaman is comparable to that of a private first class in the Army or a lance corporal in the Marines. Above the seaman ratings are six grades of noncommissioned officers—all using the term *petty officer*. Lowest of these is petty officer 3rd class, followed by 2nd class, 1st class, chief petty officer, senior chief petty officer, and master chief petty officer. The petty officer 3rd class is comparable to an Army corporal. Higher levels are of a grade similar to the various rankings of sergeants, with the master chief petty officer being on the same level as a staff sergeant major.

Basic training for recruits is conducted at a naval training center located in Great Lakes, Ill. After basic training, recruits enter areas of specialization in which they will work during their terms of service. Among the many occupational fields are marine engineering, ship maintenance, weapons control, data systems, construction, health care, logistics, cryptology, communications,

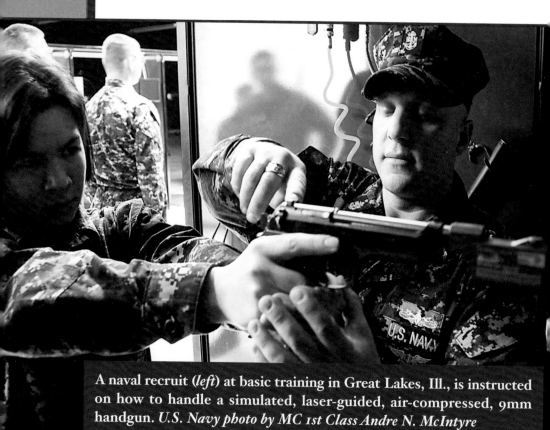

A naval recruit (*left*) at basic training in Great Lakes, Ill., is instructed on how to handle a simulated, laser-guided, air-compressed, 9mm handgun. *U.S. Navy photo by MC 1st Class Andre N. McIntyre*

intelligence, and aviation-sensor operations. In addition, within these fields are dozens of specialties, including air-traffic controller, boiler technician, electrician's mate, gunner's mate, hospital corpsman, mineman, missile technician, radioman, signalman, and sonar technician.

Chief warrant officers are specialized and commissioned career positions for which chief petty officers may apply. There are

UNITED STATES NAVAL ACADEMY

The United States Naval Academy is a public military institution of higher education in Annapolis, Maryland. It is also called Annapolis Academy. The academy prepares young people to enter the lowest commissioned ranks of the United States Navy and Marine Corps. Established as a five-year school in 1845 by Secretary of the Navy George Bancroft, it became a four-year college in 1851. The program has been shortened during wartime in order to turn out more officers for service. The academy moved briefly from Annapolis to Newport, Rhode Island, during the American Civil War. The Annapolis campus, known as "the Yard," has been a National Historic Site since 1963. The academy began accepting women in 1976.

Enrollment consists of more than 4,000 students, most of whom are male. New students must be United States citizens between the ages of 17 and 22 with exceptional physical fitness. They must also be unmarried, not pregnant, and without dependent children. Admission is very competitive, and applicants need a nomination from either a member of Congress, the U.S. president or vice president, or one of several other sources. Most accepted applicants enter the academy directly after high school, but some reserve and enlisted military personnel are also accepted.

All students, who are ranked as midshipmen, live in a dormitory complex. Students are divided into companies led by outstanding seniors. The

Football players from the United States Naval Academy playing their rivals from the United States Military Academy at the Army-Navy Game, a much-anticipated event that takes place annually. *U.S. Navy photo by MC 1st Class Chad J. McNeeley*

government pays for room, board, medical and dental care, and tuition. In addition, each midshipman gets a monthly salary to use for books, uniforms, equipment, and personal items. In return, students have to fulfill a military commitment after graduation. Graduates become ensigns in the United States Navy or second lieutenants in the United States Marine Corps. A select group of graduates can attend medical school to prepare for careers as United States Navy doctors.

Other students can apply to certain graduate schools after two years of commissioned service. Many attend the Naval Postgraduate School in Monterey, California.

The academic calendar is divided into semesters, and students also attend during the summer. Midshipmen spend the first summer before the start of classes learning the fundamentals of military life and getting into top physical condition. They spend the following summers at sea. The faculty is made up of both military officers and civilians. Students earn bachelor's degrees in such disciplines as engineering, computer science, physical science, mathematics, naval architecture, English, history, economics, political science, and oceanography.

All students must participate in intercollegiate or intramural sports. The academy's varsity sports teams, nicknamed the Midshipmen, compete in Division I of the National Collegiate Athletic Association (NCAA). The football team plays in the Football Bowl Subdivision. A highlight of the year is the annual Army-Navy football game. School colors are navy blue and gold.

four grades of chief warrant officers, with progressions through those grades depending on technical expertise, experience, and leadership ability. The Army, Marine Corps, and Air Force also have the warrant officer rank.

The other commissioned officers range from ensign to admiral of the fleet. An ensign is comparable to a second lieutenant in the Army. The rank is followed by lieutenant junior grade, lieutenant, lieutenant commander, commander, captain, rear admiral (lower half), rear admiral (upper half), vice admiral, admiral, and fleet admiral. The ranks from rear admiral lower half to admiral are equivalent to brigadier general, major general, lieutenant general, and general in the Army. A fleet admiral is equal to a five-star general.

The designation admiral is derived from the Arabic *amir-al bahr*, meaning "commander of the sea." The division into the ranks of admiral, vice admiral, and rear admiral occurred in the 17th century when English fleets were divided into squadrons of ships. The lead squadron was commanded by the admiral, the second by the vice admiral, and the last by the rear admiral. The admirals' ships were outfitted with distinctive flags, and the admirals were thus known as flag officers.

In today's Navy, officers who are entitled to assume command of ships are called line officers. The others are staff officers, who are specialists in such fields as medicine, dentistry, chaplaincy, and supply. These specialties fall under the classification of logistics.

FROM GALLEY TO SHIP OF THE LINE: NAVIES FROM ANCIENT TIMES TO C. 1850

Naval warfare has been a history of technological change from 3000 BCE to the present. Changes include the way ships are built, how they are powered, and the use of firepower. As technology has changed, so, too, have the tactics navies use to win battles. The long history of navies may be divided into three periods: the age of the galley, the age of sail, and the age of steam and steel (including nuclear power).

AGE OF THE GALLEY

The longest period in the history of navies was the age of the galley. It lasted from about 3000 BCE until the Battle of Lepanto in 1571 CE, more than 4,500 years. The warship of the time was the galley, a long seagoing vessel propelled by oars. Galleys also carried sails for cruising, but oarsmen were needed to power the ships in battle for speed and the ability to change direction quickly.

Commercial ships of the ancient world were called round ships: they were broader in relation to their length than galleys in order to hold as much cargo as possible. Early Egyptian galleys had elevated decks fore and aft for archers and spear throwers. Eventually planks were installed along the gunwales—the upper edges of a boat's side—to protect the rowers. A small platform was sometimes installed on top of the mast to accommodate archers.

GREEK GALLEYS

The first galleys had a bank of oars on each side called a unireme. (*Remus* is the Latin word for "oar.") The bireme, probably devised by the Phoenicians and adopted by the Greeks during the 8th century BCE, had two banks of oars on each side. The banks were staggered so that the oars of the upper bank cleared the oars of the lower bank. Greek biremes were about 80 feet (24 meters) long. Within a century the trireme had become the preferred galley. It had a single mast for sail. By the 5th century, when Greek triremes went into battle against the Persians, they were about 125 feet (38 m) long. They carried about 200 oarsmen, officers, and seamen with a small band of heavily armed marines.

It became virtually impossible to add more banks of rowers without making a ship unimaginably large. The problem was solved by adding rowers to oars already in place or by increasing both the number of oars and rowers. Macedonia built an 18-bank galley. This ship required 1,800 rowers, but it does not mean that there were 18 banks of oars stacked atop one another. The number of banks came to represent the number of

An ancient Greek trireme. *Hulton Archive/Getty Images*

rowers, or manpower, just as motor vehicles are rated by horsepower today.

Greek naval tactics were fairly uncomplicated. Opposing lines of galleys drew up side by side. Each side tried to overwhelm the other by ramming and boarding. Rams were attached to the prows of galleys at or below the waterline. Gangways were built at deck level from front to rear. When an enemy ship was rammed, the marines used the gangway to rush on board for hand-to-hand combat. Archers provided close-in fire. By the 5th century BCE Greek commanders had begun driving through the enemy's line to attack from the rear.

Early in the 3rd century BCE the Macedonian king Demetrius I Poliorcetes installed stone-throwing machines and catapults for hurling heavy darts. These devices were later adopted by the Romans. The weapons enabled galleys to begin combat at a greater range before ramming and boarding.

ROMAN SEA POWER

By the start of the 3rd century, Carthage had become the major Mediterranean sea power. At the same time Rome was emerging as the

BATTLE OF MYLAE

The Battle of Mylae in 260 BCE was a conflict in the First Punic War. It was the first of three sea battles in which the Romans defeated the naval power of Carthage, whose navy had been harassing Roman peninsular and Sicilian coastal towns. At Mylae the Romans destroyed 50 Carthaginian ships, and the remainder of the enemy fleet fled. The battle marked Rome's attainment of dominance in Sicilian waters by turning sea skirmishes into land battles through the use of boarding bridges that doubled as grappling irons. The Romans closed in on the enemy ships and lowered a spiked galley to hold them fast and allow their marines to board. With the help of these devices, Roman soldiers could both board enemy ships and engage in hand-to-hand fighting. Rome was established as the controlling sea power in the Mediterranean. The Roman fleet was commanded by Gen. Gaius Duilius.

leading land power. In their conflicts, called the Punic Wars, Rome had to become a naval power as well. In doing so Rome took its land tactics to sea through the use of the grappling hook and gangplank. Roman captains rammed their opponents, dropped the gangplank, and sent their marines on board the enemy galley.

After the end of the Punic Wars in 201 BCE, Rome remained for centuries the supreme naval power in the Mediterranean. By the time the Western Empire ended in the 5th century CE, the main fighting ship was a small galley called a liburnian. Probably developed originally by pirates as a fast-moving unireme, the Romans added to it a second bank of oars.

The liburnian became the standard warship of the Eastern, or Byzantine, Empire. Eventually the term came to signify any warship, however large. Heavier liburnians bore the brunt of battle, while the lighter, single-bank ships were used as scouts and cruisers—high-speed fighting ships. Throughout the 1,000 years of the Byzantine Empire, little change was made in the galley. There were improvements, however, in firepower. Missile-launching weapons grew in size. Some of them could hurl projectiles weighing 1,000 pounds (450 kilograms) as far as 750 yards (686 m).

The most fascinating weapon the Byzantines used was Greek fire. This was a combustible material made of a combination of pitch, oil, charcoal, sulfur, phosphorus, and saltpeter. It had much the same effect

Καιαὐτίοςαταχέιων προσ τασ προσεδρενό ύας τῇ πόλει δυνάμεισ· ἐ πάνεισὶ· Καὶ γράμμα τοπέ
μ οι τεέλλωνἀπανταχν· ἐπεφήμιζεν ώ σεὶ μερικηκασότπεροικήν· Καὶὁπερέι χεκαὶ ταμίμε
λα δ ανα ϊτικ ον· ταλε ωσέκελευεν ἀνάπτήραι· ὡσ αὐτῶν κατα παγα παν θ εξόμεροσ προλα δὲτ
καὶ τὸμεγγωικὸν εὐθυ πλοκ ὰ σ ταχέ ωσἀφαρεται· Καὶ πὼ χωρί σ προσορμίζεταιπὸβρύ
ὗ σοντ· ἐκ τῶ ντρ ιῶ κον τα καὶ τριακόσια σου νιὗἁμερον πλ οῖων· πολεμικῶ ν πεκαὶ ταφρ ῶ ν· οἰ
δὲ τῶ ν βασιλικ οὗ σ όλ ου κα παρ χον τεσ· τὴ ν τ ούτων ἐπάμ ο κοπέσέ λ θον· μ υκ τ οσέ ὶ π ῆ περ ται μ αν
λο χ ὁ ν τ ι τ οῖσ έ ραρπ ίοισ· Καὶ τὰ φησ ὶ ω κα τα λη ξάμ γοι· πολλ αῖσ μὲ ρ ωδρα ὑ τ ἀ ν δρ ομ ἔ σ χ ορ
π ρ ην ικ ῶ ν· Ἡ α π ὸ δ ἐ κ αὶ τὸ σ κα λαδ ἐ πῆ ρ πο λο ὑ πῆ π ὑρ

τ ό λ ε σ ρ ω μ α ί π ρ τ π ο λ   τ ο ν τ ω ν ἐ ν α ν τ ί ω ν·

Ὀ λ ί χ ω ν τ α ἡ π λ ω ό σ έ ω ν χ ρ ο μ έ ν ω ν τ ο ὑ π ά λ οισ· Καὶ πρόσ τ ὸ ν κ ό λπ ον τ ο ὑ ν β λ αρ ι ῶ ν κα τ α ρα ι ἐ σ ἐ|

as modern napalm. It was fired from tubes placed in the bows of galleys, and on reaching its destination it was difficult to extinguish. Water only helped to spread the fire. Greek fire was successfully used against Muslim fleets from the 7th century CE. Its deadliness was one reason the Byzantine Empire endured as long as it did. The formula for making Greek fire was so closely guarded that its exact components are still unknown.

VIKINGS

As the Byzantine Empire was declining and the rest of Europe was without a real power center, the Scandinavians became the great sea power of the north. The Viking galley was built with overlapping planks (a type of construction called clinker-built), put together with iron nails and caulked with tarred rope to keep out water. Both ends of the ship were identical. By the year 1000, there were three sizes of Viking galley, depending on the number of rowers. The smallest had 40 rowers, while the largest had more than 60. The middle size, with 60 oarsmen, was most often used in battle. These ships also carried rigging for sails. The Vikings used

BATTLE OF LEPANTO

The Battle of Lepanto, which took place on Oct. 7, 1571, was the last great battle between galleys. More significantly, however, it ended the naval power of the Ottoman Empire in the Mediterranean. An alliance between Venice, Spain, Genoa, and the Italian Papal States gathered a navy under the command of the Spanish general John of Austria. After about four hours of fighting, the allies were victorious, capturing 117 galleys and thousands of men. The Turkish fleet was commanded by Ali Paşa. The encounter took place off the coast of Greece.

these ships to terrorize Northern Europe, to conquer much of the British Isles, and to sail westward to Greenland and North America. Early English warships resembled those of the Vikings.

With the commercial revival in Europe around the 13th century, fleets of galleys were built to protect trade in the Mediterranean Sea. Venice alone is estimated to have had 3,000 trading ships with enough galleys to guard them from predators—either pirates or Muslim naval squadrons. By this time control of the Mediterranean was contested by Christians and Muslims. The showdown between the two, in terms of naval power, came toward the end of the 15th century. By that time the era of the galley was nearly over.

AGE OF SAIL

Three significant changes led to the decline of the galley and the emergence of warships powered by wind and sail. The first occurred in the 13th century. Dutch seafarers devised the stern rudder. This made it possible to sail into the wind as well as with it. The second feature was the addition of more masts. By the end of the 15th century, large ships were mounted with as many as four masts and carried eight or more sails. The third major change was the addition of firepower. Gunpowder had come into use in Europe in the 14th century, and its use in land battles was immediately followed by use at sea.

The mounting of guns on sailing ships had a dramatic effect on battle formation. Since the guns were aligned in one or more banks along the sides of ships, it no longer made sense for the ships to go into battle side by side as galleys normally had done. To gain effective firepower against an enemy, ships aligned in a column called the line ahead.

Line-ahead battle, also called ship-of-the-line warfare, was developed by the English Navy in the 17th century. The effectiveness of line-ahead warfare was enhanced by the broadside—the simultaneous firing of guns arrayed along the side of a ship.

In this formation the ships of the line positioned themselves one after another at intervals of about 100 yards (91 m) for a distance that could stretch as long as 12 miles (19 km). By maintaining the line throughout a battle, the fleet could function as a unit under the control of its admiral.

This formal battle line was adhered to by the British well into the 18th century despite opposition of those who defended the traditional melee-type battle in which ships went for direct confrontation with the enemy. By the end of the 18th century, the advantages of a melee were recognized to the extent that an admiral allowed breaking the line for a general chase after the enemy.

TRANSITION FROM GALLEY TO SHIP OF THE LINE

Henry VII of England created the first true battle fleet. His ships carried many guns, but most of them were small and were carried on deck. Henry VIII introduced the construction of gunports below deck and along the length of the ship. This made possible the true heavy-gun ship. His best-known warship, the *Henry Grace à Dieu*, carried 186 guns.

The appearance of the large man-of-war did not immediately displace the galley. Some types of galley continued in service well into the 19th century. During the 18th century both Sweden and Russia used galleys, including oar-powered gunboats. The United States used oar-driven gunboats in both the War of 1812 and the Mexican War.

The transitional ships between the galley and the ship of the line were the caravel, carrack, and galleon. The caravel was first designed by the Portuguese. It was a sailing ship with from one to four masts, either decked or undecked, and steered with a rudder. Two of the three ships on which Christopher Columbus and his crew sailed to the New World, the *Niña* and the *Pinta*, were caravels.

The carrack was a larger round-hulled ship with both a forecastle and aftercastle. It was based on the construction of merchant ships, but designers added stronger wooden masts, greater sail area, and broadside guns. The warships of Henry VII and Henry VIII were carracks, the predecessors of galleons.

The galleon was a modification of the carrack. Devised by the English, it was longer and narrower, with a ratio for four or five to one of length to beam (width). The forecastle was omitted or modified to enable the ship to sail into the wind more easily. The three or four masts carried square and fore and aft sails. One or two tiers of guns were carried broadside. The larger size of the galleon

The HMS *Ark Royal*, an English galleon that served as the English flagship in Britain's battle against the Spanish Armada and other naval engagements. *De Agostini Picture Library/Getty Images*

made it possible to carry larger numbers of cannons on board. These were mounted on the lower deck. The cannons were used by the British for long-range firing to do the greatest damage to enemy ships. The galleon was the main English fighting ship in the contest with the Spanish Armada. As galleon design improved, ships became longer, sailed lower in the water, and accommodated more guns broadside. Some carried as many as three tiers of cannons. Such firepower made it possible for the English to engage in ship-smashing tactics instead of the conventional ramming and boarding of the age of the galley.

SHIP OF THE LINE

The emergence of the ship of the line was gradual, and it represented primarily a change in naval tactics, not ship design. As fleet size grew, commanders realized that the oceangoing brawl called melee had become unworkable. Instead, fleets were organized into squadrons, and ships were rated according to firepower. The English Navy established six ratings. The first was for ships carrying 100 guns or more. The

The gun deck of the USS *Constitution*, one of the first frigates built for the United States Navy. *Yale Joel/Time & Life Pictures/Getty Images*

sixth-rate ships carried 18 or more. Ships of the first three ratings were considered powerful enough to be in the line of battle, a formation that became fixed during the Anglo-Dutch Wars of the 17th century. Ships of the fourth rate were used as cruisers and those of the lowest two rates as frigates.

Frigates were fast, three-masted ships carrying more than 20 guns. As their size increased, they carried up to 50 guns. A frigate carried its main battery on a single gun deck with other guns on the forecastle and quarterdeck. A classic example of the frigate is the United States Navy's *Constitution*, preserved in Boston, Mass.

The first-rate ship of the line was a 2,000-ton ship that carried a crew of about 850. The ship was built of oak with sides at least 22 inches (56 centimeters) thick. The largest ships of the line had three decks carrying cannons that could fire 42-pound (19-kilogram) shot.

From the late 18th through the early 19th century, the ship of the line that proved itself most useful was a 74-gun third rater. It had adequate firepower and better speed and maneuverability than ships of the first or second rate. Such a ship was about 175 feet (53 m) long with two gun decks. The heaviest cannons were on the lower deck, while cannons on the upper deck fired 24-pound (11-kg) shot.

THE AGE OF STEAM AND STEEL: NAVIES FROM C. 1850 TO 1945

The Industrial Revolution and the technology stemming from it permanently changed naval warfare. Steam propulsion emerged rapidly toward the end of the 18th century. The use of iron and then steel for ship construction followed. Ship design changed. Firepower, including the use of mines and torpedoes, was greatly improved, and new types of oceangoing vessels—including the submarine—appeared. The revolving turret with cannons mounted inside was introduced. The ship of the line turned into the battleship. Early in the 20th century the invention of the airplane eroded the line of battle formation. By the time of World War II, the battleship was giving way to the aircraft carrier as the heart of a fleet, and battle formation at sea was completely transformed.

STEAMSHIPS

The first steamships were paddle wheelers. The paddle wheels, however, were especially vulnerable to firepower, and if they were placed on the side of a ship, they took up room that otherwise could be used for gunports. The invention of the screw propeller in England by John Ericsson and Francis Pettit Smith, independently of each other, did away with the need for paddle wheels. The invention was rejected in England. Ericsson went to the United States and, at the insistence of Captain Robert Stockton, developed a steamer with a screw propeller. This was the *Princeton*, the first warship to have all machinery below the waterline and out of reach of conventional firepower. Britain and France soon followed with similar ships.

NEW FIREPOWER

The introduction of shell guns to replace those that fired round shot led to the use of iron plate mounted on the hulls of ships as protection against the more damaging impact of exploding shells. The French *Gloire* was the first warship protected for its entire length by wrought iron backed by wood. The British soon countered with the *Warrior*, a much larger ship. These ships went to sea in the 1850s just before the American Civil War. In that war two ironclads proved the need for such warships in the well-known battle between the Confederacy's *Merrimack* and the North's *Monitor*. The South also developed the first subsurface weapons—mines that could be detonated by contact or electrically. The first mines were called torpedoes. Later, when underwater propelled missiles

Sailors handling a torpedo on the upper deck on the HMS *Rattlesnake*, one of the torpedo gunboats of the Royal Navy. *Hulton Archive/Getty Images*

were developed, the term *torpedo* was given to them. Mines came to refer to stationary explosives placed under water.

The true torpedo was devised in Scotland after the American Civil War. As it became more accurate and a real threat in war, torpedo boats were a major menace. To counter them the torpedo-boat destroyer was developed by Britain in 1893. It carried torpedoes and quick-firing guns and was intended to accompany a battle line at sea.

BATTLESHIPS

The ironclad ships, with their center-mounted gun turrets, led directly to the creation of the battleship. Studies of naval combat in the Spanish-American and Russo-Japanese wars indicated that fire from larger, long-range guns was more effective than close-in firing from smaller weapons. Improved gunsights, new spotting techniques, and range finders made long-range gunnery practicable. The first true battleship was the British *Dreadnought*, launched in 1906. It had ten 12-inch (30-cm) guns and could reach a speed of 21 knots (a knot is one nautical mile per hour).

The battleship played a pivotal role in World War I. Without it the Allies could have lost control of the seas and, therefore, the war. This was prevented by the Battle of Jutland in May 1916, the single large-scale clash of battleships of the war. The British kept the German Navy bottled up in the Baltic and North seas, forcing Germany to rely on unrestricted submarine warfare. By the end of the war the Allies had developed adequate countermeasures, but German U-boats sent to the bottom of the sea 5,234 merchant ships, 10 battleships, 18 cruisers, 20 destroyers, and 9 submarines from the Allies' arsenal.

AIRCRAFT AND AIRCRAFT CARRIERS

Control of the seas is now accomplished by use of aircraft in conjunction with ships and submarines. In November 1910, the USS *Birmingham*, a scout cruiser, launched the first airplane ever to take off from a ship. Two months later an airplane landed on an improvised flight deck on the USS *Pennsylvania*, an armored cruiser in San Francisco Bay. By the start of World War I the British Admiralty had converted steamers to carry seaplanes. The first true aircraft carrier, at least in appearance, was the converted British passenger liner *Argus*. It had a flight deck extending from bow to stern that

Sopwith Camel planes on the HMS *Furious*, a cruiser that was modified to carry aircraft during World War I. *Hulton Archive /Getty Images*

could both launch and land planes. By 1915, the Royal Navy had seaplanes that could launch torpedo attacks against ships.

To counter air attack, it was necessary to modify a ship's firepower. The turret battery provided gunfire that could be aimed at all sides of a ship. To hit aircraft demanded rapid-fire, high-angle guns. American battleships soon adopted antiaircraft guns and machine guns to fire at attacking planes.

As soon as World War I was over, several nations began building aircraft carriers. The Royal Navy's HMS *Hermes*, started in 1918, was the first ship designed specifically to be an aircraft carrier. Although they featured a wide, flat deck, they also had an island, or bridge, for command and navigation. Most of the carriers manufactured by Britain, France, Japan, and the United States after the war saw action in World War II.

During World War II, carriers played a decisive role, particularly in the Pacific battles of Midway, the Coral Sea, and Leyte Gulf. As a result battle formation at sea was altered. The task force emerged, consisting of three or four carriers in the center, surrounded by six or seven battleships and cruisers and 13 or 14 destroyers. The destroyers gave

THE BATTLE OF LEYTE GULF

The Battle of Leyte Gulf (Oct. 23–26, 1944) was fought in the Philippines and was the decisive air and sea battle of the Pacific during World War II. It was also the greatest naval battle ever fought.

The battle was precipitated by a U.S. amphibious assault on the central Philippine island of Leyte on Oct. 20. The Japanese responded with Sho-Go (Victory Operation), a plan to decoy the U.S. Third Fleet north, away from the San Bernardino Strait, while converging three forces on Leyte Gulf to attack the landing; the First Attack Force was to move from the north across the Sibuyen Sea through the San Bernardino Strait, with the Second Attack Force and C Force moving from the south across the Mindanao Sea through the Surigao Strait.

As the Japanese forces moved into position southwest of Leyte, submarines of the U.S. Seventh Fleet discovered the First Attack Force and sank two heavy cruisers west of Palawan on Oct. 23. A series of almost continuous surface and air clashes followed, especially in the Sibuyen Sea, while the U.S. Third Fleet chased the Japanese decoy. Finally, on Oct. 25, the three major engagements of the battle were fought, almost simultaneously. At the Surigao Strait, battleships and cruisers from the Seventh Fleet destroyed C Force and forced the Second Attack Force to withdraw. Meanwhile, the First Attack Force passed through the unguarded San Bernardino Strait and inflicted heavy damage on the Seventh Fleet escort carriers off Samar but withdrew

American troops aboard landing barges look up during the Battle of Leyte Gulf. American and Japanese planes fought overhead in what was a decisive air and sea battle of World War II. © *AP Images*

unexpectedly just as they seemed ready to attack the landing operations. In the north, off Cape Engaño, part of the Third Fleet sank Japanese carriers while another part moved south, attacking and pursuing the First Attack Force.

A total of 244 ships were involved. The battle so crippled the Japanese that the American Armed Forces were able to invade the Philippines.

antisubmarine protection and provided an outer ring of antiaircraft fire. The battleships and cruisers provided protection from surface enemies and gave antiaircraft protection closer to the carriers. The introduction of radar fire control and the proximity fuze made it virtually impossible for enemy aircraft to approach the carriers.

SIGNIFICANT NAVAL ENGAGEMENTS SINCE THE SECOND WORLD WAR

Although the world has avoided another global conflict since World War II, nearly every decade since then has seen a significant outbreak of hostilities involving at least some of the major powers, and naval forces have been involved each time.

Each successive conflict has given the United States and other large nations an opportunity to renew their practice of naval combat tactics and test new equipment. A history of those conflicts helps trace the development of those tactics and equipment, and reinforces the continued importance of naval strength in modern warfare.

KOREAN WAR

From a 21st-century perspective, the Korean War may seem like a stalemate that still haunts the modern world, given North Korea's unpredictable nuclear belligerence.

However, as unsatisfactory as the long-standing division of North and South Korea may seem now, it was preferable to what was predicted to be the probable outcome when that conflict started—a Korea entirely under communist control. The United States Navy played a pivotal role in preventing that outcome.

Korea was divided at the 38th Parallel as a result of an agreement between the United States and the Soviet Union at the end of World War II. On June 25, 1950, North Korean forces invaded South Korea. Within

Vice Admiral C. Turner Joy stepping out of a tent after attending a cease-fire conference on the Korean War. *Keystone/Hulton Archive/ Getty Images*

C. TURNER JOY

Vice Admiral Charles Turner Joy (1895–1956) was a significant figure in the United States Navy. He was born in St. Louis, Mo., and graduated from the United States Naval Academy in 1916. After going on to serve on the USS *Pennsylvania*, he earned a graduate degree and later served in China as part of the Navy's Yangtze Patrol and held other assignments in East Asia as well.

Joy, who directed U.S. naval forces and coordinated efforts with United Nations (UN) forces during the first two years of the Korean War, had a wide-ranging perspective on the Korean conflict. In more than 30 years of experience in the United States Navy previously, he already had faced the two other great powers of the Pacific Rim: first in the Pacific Fleet against Japan during World War II, and later conducting naval operations in support of the Nationalist Chinese in their struggle against the communists who were taking control of the mainland.

In 1950, the outbreak of the Korean War would bring Joy into action against North Korea. As Commander of Naval Forces, Far East, Joy was responsible for establishing and protecting sea lanes to supply U.S. forces on the Korean Peninsula. Then ships and marines under Joy's command made possible the bold counterattack at Inch'ŏn.

Joy's perspective on the Korean War was broadened when he was named the senior UN delegate to the Korean Armistice Conference. He later concluded his long and varied career by serving as superintendent of the U.S. Naval Academy.

days, the South Korean capital had fallen, and South Korea's remaining military forces, supported by U.S. troops, were in retreat.

The Navy's role in turning the tide of this conflict was three-fold. The first was to maintain a defensive presence around other sensitive areas of the Pacific Rim, such as Formosa and the Philippines. The second was to stop North Korean naval operations against the South. The third was to facilitate a dramatic landing at Inch'ŏn, so U.S. forces could strike back at the middle of the country rather than be confined to fighting from a limited portion of the south.

It was this last operation that was the turning point in driving North Korean forces back north of the 38th Parallel, where they remain today.

SUEZ CRISIS

The Suez Crisis served as an early demonstration of the multifaceted role a modern navy could play in an isolated conflict, even though the outcome was ultimately limited by political considerations.

The Suez Canal is a crucial maritime link for the transportation of oil from the

Sailors look up at a Royal Navy helicopter hovering above during the Suez Crisis. *Popperfoto/Getty Images*

Middle East, since it is part of the only direct water route between the Arabian and Mediterranean seas. The canal had been under international operation, but in July of 1956, Egypt nationalized it. French and British forces mobilized, ostensibly to aid the Israelis in a conflict against the Egyptians, but with the underlying objective of taking control of the Suez Canal.

Anglo-French naval forces quickly took effective control of the eastern Mediterranean Sea, and then were instrumental in an invasion of the canal zone—first by ship-to-shore bombardment and carrier-based air attacks, and then by amphibious landings. Their forces were soon establishing control of the canal.

Successful though it was militarily, the Anglo-French action was unpopular internationally, especially in the context of Cold War tensions. Ultimately, the geopolitical situation forced the British and French to forego the military advantage they had achieved, and the Suez Canal would pass into Egyptian hands. However, the incident remained a demonstration of how modern naval forces could provide seaborne, air, and amphibious support to a concentrated military objective.

VIETNAM WAR

Though the Vietnam War ended in defeat for the United States, it serves as an illustration of the operational flexibility that would be required of the United States Navy in the late 20th century and beyond.

As a practical matter, U.S. naval operations in Vietnam were divided into what were referred to as the "blue water" and "brown water" navies. The blue water navy was the ocean-going fleet. From their offshore position, aircraft carriers of the blue water navy could provide air support of troop operations onshore, as well as act as a base for bombing missions. The blue water navy also provided ship-to-shore bombardment and fulfilled a vital supply role for U.S. forces.

The brown water navy operated on the inland waterways of Vietnam. There, they could disrupt the movement of enemy troops and supplies through the country, while also helping keep U.S. ground forces supplied. They also fought in support of those troops in actions taking place near those inland waterways.

An additional role for the United States Navy in Vietnam was performed by Naval

Mobile Construction Battalions, popularly known as the "Seabees." The Seabees undertook engineering and construction projects, both to create military infrastructure and to provide facilities for Vietnam's civilian population.

Overall, the Vietnam War helped illustrate how the Navy's role in modern warfare had shifted from fighting great naval battles to performing a wide variety of smaller, tactical missions.

PUEBLO INCIDENT

The USS *Pueblo*, a Navy intelligence ship, and its 83 crewmen, was captured by North Korean patrol boats off the coast of North Korea on Jan. 23, 1968. The United States, maintaining that the *Pueblo* had been in international waters, began a military buildup in the area. It also initiated negotiations that resulted in an agreement that secured the release of the 82 surviving crewmen (one died from wounds suffered during the capture) on Dec. 23, 1968. The agreement allowed the United States to publicly disavow the confession

The USS *Pueblo* at sea. © *AP Images*

the crew had signed, admitting the ship's intrusion, apologizing, pledging to cease all future action, and acknowledging the truth of confessions obtained during captivity. A naval inquiry into these confessions and the actions of Comdr. Lloyd M. Bucher produced no apparent disciplinary action.

NAVIES IN THE MODERN AGE

T hroughout the Cold War, the world's two largest navies belonged to the Soviet Union and the United States. With the breakup of the Soviet Union, the United States was left as the clear number one, though Russia still has a considerable naval force. More recently though, a third navy has been rising quickly, and today China's Navy is second only to the United States Navy in manpower.

Below is a description of the major types of ships commonly seen in the world's navies. Different countries use different types of vessels, but the range of craft is generally similar to the descriptions below, which are based on the equipment of the United States Navy.

COMBAT VESSELS

Major classes of combat vessels include aircraft carriers, amphibious assault ships, attack submarines, ballistic missile submarines, cruisers, and destroyers. A traditional type of combat vessel, called a frigate, is receiving reduced emphasis by the United States Navy, while a newer type of vessel, known as a littoral combat ship, is factoring more heavily in naval plans.

The once-dominant class known as the battleship saw its role diminished by the advantages of the aircraft carrier, and construction of them ceased in 1945 with the end of World War II. The few remaining battleships continued to see action into the 1980s, but the last active-duty battleship, the USS *New Jersey*, was decommissioned in 1991.

Aircraft Carriers

By the mid-2010s, the United States Navy possessed 10 aircraft carriers, all of them nuclear-powered. With the deactivation of the USS *Enterprise* in late 2012, all of the active-duty United States Navy aircraft carriers were members of the Nimitz class. These 97,000-ton ships can accommodate a total crew (including air wing) of over 5,000, and have a top speed in excess of 30 knots. These ships are 1,092 feet (333 m) long and

USS *ENTERPRISE*

The USS *Enterprise* is the first nuclear-powered aircraft carrier, launched in 1960 and commissioned by the United States Navy in 1961. Powered by eight nuclear reactors (two for each of its four propellers), the *Enterprise*—displacing about 75,000 tons and having a flight deck of 1,101 by 252 feet (336 by

The inactivation ceremony of the USS *Enterprise* in December 2012. *U.S. Navy photo by MC 2nd Class Nick C. Scott*

77 m)—cruised more than 200,000 miles (320,000 km) over three years before requiring refueling. In addition to endurance, its nuclear reactors gave the ship greater space for aviation fuel, ordnance, and stores—important advantages over oil-powered carriers. With a top speed of more than 30 knots, in its time it was said to be the fastest warship afloat. The *Enterprise* saw active duty for over 50 years before being deactivated in late 2012 in preparation for decommissioning.

have a flight deck that is 252 feet (77 m) wide. Beginning in 2015, the United States Navy will replace the Nimitz class with a more modern class of aircraft carriers, the Gerald R. Ford class.

Subsequent to vast improvements in military helicopters, the Navy converted some World War II carriers into helicopter carriers for amphibious assault. Marines, instead of simply landing and fighting their way inland, can use helicopters to get to the rear of hostile beach defenses. The success of these carriers resulted in the commissioning of the USS *Iwo Jima* in 1961 as the first ship designed as a helicopter carrier. This and similar ships can each carry a Marine battalion with guns, vehicles, equipment, and a helicopter squadron to fly them ashore. This type of ship is now classed as an amphibious assault ship and is playing a growing role in today's Navy.

ATTACK SUBMARINES

The United States Navy has over 50 attack submarines, all of them nuclear-powered. Most of these attack submarines are in the Los Angeles class, though by 2013 the Navy had begun to introduce the Virginia class, which it considers to be the next generation of attack submarines.

The main job of attack submarines is to target enemy shipping and other submarines. Attack submarines carry torpedoes and depth charges, and some carry missiles to launch against surface craft. Submarines are also used for surveillance, reconnaissance, landing-force support, laying mines, and rescue missions.

BALLISTIC MISSILE SUBMARINES

Ballistic missile submarines have given the Navy a moveable and difficult-to-detect

IC PARTS OF A BALLISTIC-MISSILE SUBMARINE

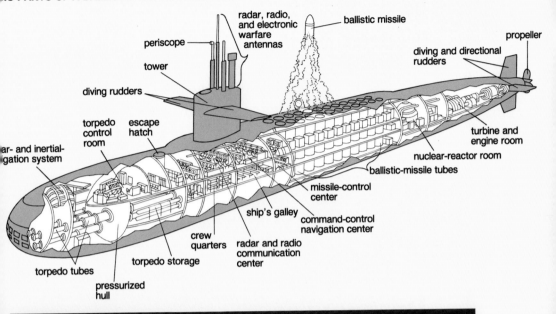

radar, radio, and electronic warfare antennas

periscope

tower

diving rudders

ballistic missile

propeller

diving and directional rudders

torpedo control room

escape hatch

ar- and inertial-igation system

turbine and engine room

nuclear-reactor room

ballistic-missile tubes

missile-control center

ship's galley

command-control navigation center

crew quarters

radar and radio communication center

torpedo storage

torpedo tubes

pressurized hull

An artist's rendition of an Ohio-class ballistic missile submarine shows 24 missile tubes for housing Trident I missiles. The ships are 560 feet (171 meters) in length. Each missile floats to the water surface before it is activated and has a range of 4,350 miles (7,000 kilometers). Driven by a large, water-cooled reactor and steam turbines, the ship can exceed speeds of 200 knots. *Encyclopædia Britannica, Inc.*

launch platform for ballistic missiles. Since the 1960s, this capability has been viewed as a key strategic deterrence against an attack on the United States. Currently, the United States Navy has 14 ballistic missile submarines, all of them belonging to the Ohio class. These vessels have a submerged displacement of 18,750 tons and are 560 feet (171 m) in length.

CRUISERS

Cruisers are equipped with weaponry to attack air, sea, underwater, and land-based combatants. This flexibility allows them to operate as part of a carrier battle group, support amphibious forces, or function independently. They carry crews of about 330, and measure 567 feet (173 m) long by 55 feet (17 m) wide. Their gas turbine propulsion systems give them top speeds in excess of 30 knots.

DESTROYERS

Modern destroyers are designed for maximum functional flexibility. By 2013, the Navy had over 60 destroyers, all belonging to the Arleigh Burke class. These destroyers are 509 feet (155 m) long by 59 feet (18 m) wide and carry crews of about 275. Their gas turbine engines give them a top speed in excess of 30 knots, and their combat capability is based around the Aegis Combat System. This system coordinates sophisticated radar with a Tomahawk missile system.

FRIGATES AND LITTORAL COMBAT SHIPS

At 445 feet (134 m) long and 45 feet (14 m) wide, frigates are basically scaled-down versions of destroyers. With technology making destroyers more versatile, and with the complexity of modern warfare putting a premium on operational flexibility, the Navy has decreased its emphasis on frigates over the years, and by the mid-2010s the number of them in operation was down to 23.

Picking up some of the operational load from frigates in the years ahead will be a new category of vessels called littoral combat ships. These are a little smaller than frigates and built to move swiftly, with a top speed of over 40 knots. They are also designed to be reconfigured quickly with different payloads called mission packages, which allow them to adapt their operational capabilities to the situation. This emphasis on speed and flexibility is seen as necessary to meet the unpredictable challenges of modern warfare.

Amphibious Warfare Ships

The term *amphibious* refers to the place where land and sea meet. The word is a biological term that means the ability to live in water and on land. Amphibious vessels are mainly assault ships, especially when landings are carried out by combined Navy and Marine Corps teams. There are seven types of assault ships. Most are used to land combat troops and equipment on hostile territory.

The United States pioneered the development of amphibians during World War II. They were used in the D-Day landings in Normandy in June 1944, as well as throughout the Pacific campaigns against Japanese-held islands. The best known is the Tank Landing Ship, or LST, of which the United States originally built 1,041.

Today, amphibious operations are based around large, multi-capability amphibious assault ships, which can act as a base for a variety of smaller vehicles. Because of their operational flexibility, amphibious assault ships have been playing a growing role in the United States Navy, and by 2013 the Navy had 11 of them in active duty. Most of these

The USS *Essex*, a Wasp-class amphibious assault ship of the United States Navy, in formation with the Essex Amphibious Ready Group in the Andaman Sea. *U.S. Navy photo by Chief MC Ty Swartz*

belong to the Wasp class, which are the largest amphibious craft in the world. With a length of 844 feet (253 m), a width of 106 feet (32 m), and displacement of around 41,000 tons, amphibious assault ships resemble a smaller version of aircraft carriers. Part of their flexibility stems from the ability to launch a variety of aircraft, as well as landing vessels.

Those landing vessels are smaller boats designed to get military personnel and equipment on shore. Among these smaller boats are air-cushioned landing craft, which the Navy began using in the mid-1980s. These allow a crew of just five to transport a payload of 60–75 tons at speeds in excess of 40 knots. The air-cushioned technology makes 70 percent of the world's coastline accessible to these craft, as opposed to the 15 percent that is accessible to conventional landing craft.

The more conventional landing craft used by the Navy are classified as Mechanized and Utility Uanding Craft (LCM and LCU, respectively). LCMs can be up to 74 feet (23 m) long and have a ramp in the bow for landing troops and equipment. LCUs are larger, at 135 feet (41 m). They have ramps in both the bow and the stern and are capable of operating at sea for up to 10 days.

SHIPS FOR LOGISTICS

Logistics, among other things, involves the tasks of supply and repair. The Navy has a great variety of ships devoted to these jobs. Since the fleets remain at sea for months at a time, it is necessary that fuel, food, ammunition, and other provisions be brought to them. Repairs must also be made on the ships, weapons, and other complex onboard systems.

Among the many vessels occupied with logistics are container ships that supply Navy vessels and other branches of the Armed Services; fueling ships; aviation logistical

An unmanned RQ-8A Fire Scout helicopter, one of the Navy's many aircraft, preparing to land aboard the USS *Nashville*, an amphibious transport dock ship. *U.S. Navy photo by Kurt Lengfield*

support ships; cargo ships; fleet ocean tug-boats; tender ships, which carry mainly replacement parts and technicians; rescue and salvage ships; cable laying and repair ships; and many more. Some service ships—such as gasoline, oil, and water barges—remain at naval bases or are anchored in harbors. Some are self-propelled, but others must be hauled by tugs.

Aircraft

In addition to its great variety of ships, the United States Navy also has about 3,700 aircraft. These include fighters, patrol planes, antisubmarine planes, transport planes, in-flight fuelers, observation planes, trainers, early-warning planes, and helicopters.

NOTABLE NAVIES OF THE WORLD

Historically great navies have tended to be built as a function of rivalries between countries. England's long naval tradition originated as a response to its rivalries with Spain and France; the Cold War between the United States and Soviet Union led each to create the largest navies the oceans have ever seen; today, North and South Korea are examples of countries whose mutual distrust has led them to build large navies to defend their interests.

The following is a description of some of the 21st century's great navies, touching on both the naval traditions of their countries and the status of their fleets in the modern age.

CHINA

In the early 15th century, Chinese Admiral Zheng He undertook seven voyages to Southeast Asia and the Indian Ocean. His

Chinese naval officers at the Port of Qingdao in China. *Guang Niu/ Getty Images*

ships were large and sophisticated for their time, and from this beginning China might easily have become one of the early naval powers. However, economic decline led China to neglect naval affairs for centuries.

While China did have a national navy both before and after the communist revolution, it has only been since the country's economic boom that it has developed the industrial base, national wealth, and global ambitions to pursue a major campaign of naval expansion.

This new naval emphasis is focused on three goals. One is to improve surface warfare capabilities. Toward this end, China has made significant increases in its number of submarines and high-speed patrol boats capable of firing antiship cruise missiles. China is also believed to have developed the world's first antiship ballistic missile.

China's second naval emphasis has been on improving surface-to-air defenses. It has addressed this by installing mid- to long-range missile launchers on its newer ships, and by developing an advanced radar system comparable to that of the U.S. Aegis system.

The third area of emphasis in China's recent naval buildup is force projection. Toward this end, China has been building larger vessels and has increased its underway replenishment capacity, allowing its navy to undertake longer missions.

By 2012, China had built a navy with a quarter million members, second only in manpower to the United States Navy. China's Navy also boasts over 800 ships, and though most of these are small fast-attack and patrol craft, the fleet also includes 26 destroyers and an aircraft carrier.

FRANCE

France's Navy first became a credible force in the 17th century and was formed initially to pursue the dual objectives of protecting French trade routes and expanding France's colonial empire.

For decades the French Navy was over-shadowed by the Royal Navy, though the French got the upper hand in a sea battle that played a significant role in the American Revolution. When French Admiral Comte de Grasse defeated an English fleet in 1781's second Battle of the Chesapeake, the English were unable to resupply the besieged General Charles Cornwallis at Yorktown. Cornwallis subsequently was forced to surrender, which effectively ended the war.

The British decisively re-established naval dominance over the French in 1805's Battle of Trafalgar, and from that time on the French Navy has had a limited role in world affairs. However, it has a distinguished history of military innovation, dating back to the intro-duction of the world's first ironclad ship in

1859 and continuing through the launch of a high-speed destroyer in the 1920s and multiple innovations in submarine design.

Though France is cautious about becoming entangled in military alliances, it has occasionally participated in multinational military operations when it felt its interests were at stake. In the 21st century, France intervened in civil conflicts in Libya and Mali.

To pursue its military objectives, France maintains a fleet of over 150 vessels, which includes 10 submarines, 12 destroyers, and an aircraft carrier. In addition to these seagoing vehicles, the French Navy also has a Fleet Air Arm. In total, members of the French Navy number over 38,000, under the leadership of over about 4,750 officers.

NORTH KOREA

Historically the unified Korea that existed before the end of World War II was known as the "Hermit Kingdom" for its practice of keeping to itself. This national philosophy did not call for much in the way of a naval presence, and as a result, Korea had little in the way of naval history prior to the Korean War.

That war established two things that would lead to building of a large North Korean Navy. The first of these things was a continuous state of hostility and suspicion between North Korea and South Korea. At first it seemed that the Korean War would result in a rout of the South, and then it began to look like a sound defeat of the North. Ultimately, however, the conflict ended up with things looking as they did at the start of the war, with a border drawn roughly along the 38th Parallel. This has created the feeling that the conflict was left unresolved, with each side still nervously eyeing the actions of the other and building military capabilities to defend itself.

The second thing the Korean War established was how decisive naval intervention could be in a conflict fought on a peninsula. United States Navy action was decisive in turning the tide of the war, and this included supporting the amphibious landing at Inch'ŏn. Since that time, coastal defenses have been a top priority of the North Koreans.

To pursue this priority, North Korea has built a Navy that consists not of huge, oceangoing craft, but of large numbers of smaller, versatile vessels suitable for coastal defense. This force includes roughly 600 surface craft and over 80 small submarines. The staffing of this navy also represents a strength-in-numbers philosophy, as members of the North Korean Navy are estimated to number close to 60,000.

RUSSIA

The Russian Navy dates to the late 17th-century vision of Peter the Great, who sought to modernize Russia along the lines of the European powers. Part of this vision included securing Russian access to trade routes via the Baltic Sea in the north and the Black Sea in the south. To achieve that goal, Russia needed a navy to combat the dominant powers in those waters, which were Sweden in the Baltic and Turkey in the Black Sea.

Russia succeeded in establishing a presence on both seas, although conflicts with Turkey were to continue through the 18th and 19th centuries. In the late 19th century, a buildup of the Russian Navy included a Pacific Fleet that rivalled Japan's. This led to conflict and ultimately war between the two nations, and when Russia was defeated in 1905, it was a long-lasting setback for its Navy.

The Soviet era was to see two major periods of expansion for the country's Navy: first during the years leading up to World War II, and later during the Cold War. During this Cold War phase, the Soviets introduced the capability of launching nuclear weapons from their submarines, and maintaining this threat while defending against U.S. and British submarines was a major focus until the collapse of the Soviet Union in 1991.

Russian sailors at the port in the Ukranian city of Sevastopol, where the Russian Black Sea Fleet, a large unit of the Russian Navy, is stationed. *Viktor Drachev/AFP/Getty Image*

Though the remaining Russian Navy is reduced from its Soviet-era peak, it is still formidable, with personnel totaling approximately 145,000. Its fleet of more than 270 vessels features in excess of 60 submarines and 15 destroyers. Plans are also in the works for new ships, which should further add to Russia's presence as a major naval force.

SOUTH KOREA

Despite their intense political divisions, South Korea and North Korea are linked both historically and geographically, so their naval situations are fairly similar.

The historical link means that as with North Korea, South Korea does not have a long-standing naval tradition. The geographic link means that each country feels that it has an enemy right next door; therefore most of the naval emphasis has been on coastal defenses and patrol capabilities to guard against invasion by the other.

As a result, like North Korea, South Korea has built a Navy primarily around fast and maneuverable smaller craft rather than large vessels designed for long voyages. With the military backing of the United States behind it, South Korea has not had to match the huge number of boats that North Korea has. Still, the South has a fairly considerable fleet consisting of 161 surface craft and 23 submarines.

Even more impressive is the scale of manpower. Including marines, South Korea's Navy totals 87,000 members, even more than North Korea's. To put these numbers in perspective, if combined the North and South Korean naval forces would total slightly more than Russia's, making it the third biggest navy in the world. For the time being, however, those navies remain divided—and sharply focused on each other's activities.

UNITED KINGDOM

"Britannia rules the waves." This statement was true for nearly 400 years. England is part of an island. As such its chief military force became a navy instead of land-based fighting units. With its Navy Great Britain was able to defend its home island, blockade continental ports in wartime, and build a worldwide empire that endured until after World War II.

As long ago as the 9th century, Alfred the Great was able to defend the British Isles from attacking Danes and to challenge them for control of the North Sea. Under William the Conqueror in the 11th century, certain cities were given commercial privileges in exchange for providing fighting ships and men in time of war. In the 14th century Edward III led England into the Hundred Years' War with France. He created a royal navy for himself, partly to transport combat troops to the Continent.

Today's Royal Navy was founded by Henry VIII in the 16th century. He was the first monarch to build a fleet of ships designed primarily for fighting. He also created the system of naval administration that has lasted, with modifications, to the present.

The Royal Navy became England's chief means of defense and colonization during the reign of Elizabeth I. She put John Hawkins in charge of the Navy, and it was he who designed the first galleon—the ship that eventually became the ship of the line. Ships of his design defeated the Spanish Armada.

Under Oliver Cromwell in the late 17th century, the Navy was reorganized and provided with an annual budget. During the Anglo-Dutch Wars at this time, the ships of the line were divided into squadrons, and

BATTLE OF TRAFALGAR

The Battle of Trafalgar (Oct. 21, 1805) was a naval engagement of the Napoleonic Wars, which established British naval supremacy for more than 100 years; it was fought west of Cape Trafalgar, Spain, between Cádiz and the Strait of Gibraltar. A fleet of 33 ships (18 French and 15 Spanish) under Admiral Pierre de Villeneuve fought a British fleet of 27 ships under Admiral Horatio Nelson.

At the end of September 1805, Villeneuve had received orders to leave Cádiz and land troops at Naples to support the French campaign in southern Italy. On October 19–20 his fleet slipped out of Cádiz, hoping to get into the Mediterranean Sea without giving battle. Nelson caught him off Cape Trafalgar on October 21.

Villeneuve ordered his fleet to form a single line heading north, and Nelson ordered his fleet to form two squadrons and attack Villeneuve's line from the west, at right angles. By noon the larger squadron, led by Admiral Cuthbert Collingwood in the *Royal Sovereign*, had engaged the rear (south) 16 ships of the French-Spanish line. At 11:50 AM Nelson, in the *Victory*, signaled his famous message: "England expects that every man will do his duty." Then his squadron, with 12 ships, attacked the van and center of Villeneuve's line, which included Villeneuve in the *Bucentaure*. The majority of Nelson's squadron broke through and shattered Villeneuve's lines in the pell-mell battle. Six of the leading French and Spanish ships, under Admiral Pierre Dumanoir, were ignored

Lord Nelson dying at the Battle of Trafalgar in a detail from a painting by Daniel Maclise. *Time & Life Pictures/Getty Images*

in the first attack and were able to turn about to aid those behind. But Dumanoir's weak counterattack failed and was driven off. Collingwood completed the destruction of the rear, and the battle ended about 5:00 PM. Villeneuve himself was captured, and his fleet lost 19 or 20 ships—which were surrendered to the British—and 14,000 men, of whom half were prisoners of war.

Nelson was mortally wounded by a sniper, but when he died he was certain of his complete victory. About 1,500 British seamen were killed or wounded, but no British ships were lost. Trafalgar shattered forever Napoleon's plans to invade England.

the line-ahead formation was established. This line-of-battle tactic was first used in June 1666 and became official policy thereafter.

The most serious challenge to the Royal Navy prior to World War I came between 1793 and 1815—the era of the wars with France subsequent to the French Revolution and during the reign of Napoleon. France had built a larger and more powerful Navy during the 1790s. By 1809, however, the British had reestablished command of the seas with a fleet of about 1,100 vessels, including 152 ships of the line and manpower exceeding 140,000.

HORATIO NELSON

Horatio Nelson was born on Sept. 29, 1758, in Norfolk in the parish of Burnham Thorpe. He was the sixth of 11 children in a family that was genteel, scholarly, and poor. Nelson entered the navy as a midshipman at the age of 12. He became a lieutenant in 1777, and soon after, when he was only 20 years old, he was promoted to captain. He served in the West Indies in the war against the American colonies from 1777 to 1783.

When war broke out with revolutionary France in 1793, Nelson was given command of the 64-gun ship *Agamemnon*, then in the Mediterranean. He lost nearly all the sight of his right eye in 1794 in the Siege of Calvi on the island of Corsica. In 1797, he was knighted for his bold tactics in the Battle of Cape St. Vincent, and he also became a rear admiral. Later that year he lost his right arm during an assault on Santa Cruz de Tenerife in the Canary Islands.

As soon as Nelson recovered, he was sent to destroy the fleet that escorted Napoleon's invasion of Egypt. The smashing victory at the Battle of the Nile secured British control of the Mediterranean and made Nelson the hero of England.

Nelson became a vice admiral in 1801. Later that year Nelson won a notable victory over the Danish fleet at Copenhagen. In the midst of the battle his superior officer hoisted the signal to withdraw from action. Nelson put a telescope to his blind eye and said, "I really do not see the signal." He continued fighting, turning probable disaster into triumph.

After the battle, Nelson was made a viscount. He was later given command of the Mediterranean fleet. He blockaded the French fleet at Toulon for more than a year until it slipped out. Nelson chased it to the West Indies and back, laid siege to it and the allied Spanish fleet in the harbor of Cádiz, and finally brought them both to bay off Cape Trafalgar on Oct. 21, 1805. Nelson's tactics shattered the enemy fleet. Near the end of the battle, when victory was assured, Nelson fell mortally wounded. His flag captain, Thomas Hardy, carried him below deck. He died on Oct. 21, 1805. Nelson was greatly mourned in Britain, where he had been extremely popular. By destroying the combined French and Spanish fleets at Trafalgar, he secured the supremacy of British naval power for more than 100 years.

After the Napoleonic wars the size of the Royal Navy decreased, though sufficient strength was kept to maintain the empire. No serious threat was posed to Britain until Germany began building a large navy early in the 20th century. At that time, the leading European powers—significantly influenced by the ideas of the American Alfred T. Mahan—began upgrading their navies along with the United States.

During World War I, Britain managed to keep the German Navy at bay after the otherwise indecisive Battle of Jutland in 1916. Attention was then turned to dealing with Germany's unrestricted use of submarine warfare. This problem was solved by developing the convoy system of shipping so that individual transport and other vessels, protected by destroyers, could not be picked off one by one. Naval aviation was established during the war. The Fleet Air Arm was given control of all seaborne aircraft by 1937.

After World War II, the Royal Navy was second only to the United States Navy in size and power, though it was later overtaken by the Navy of the Soviet Union. The Royal Navy took part in the Korean War and in naval

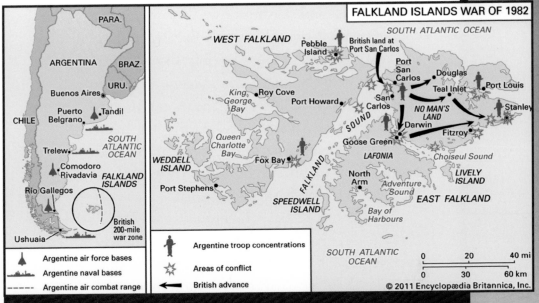

The Falkland Islands War zone (*left*) and the route of British landing forces (*right*). *Encyclopædia Britannica, Inc.*

actions throughout the Commonwealth. In 1982, it successfully took part in the Falkland Islands War. Today, the Royal Navy's duties are partially integrated into the combined forces of the North Atlantic Treaty Organization (NATO). It has been given responsibility for nuclear deterrence and maintains a fleet of nuclear-armed submarines.

In the 21st century, Great Britain's naval mission is less ambitious than when it sought to extend an empire around the world, but that mission is no less complex. The remnants of that empire have left British territorial possessions and Commonwealth members spread around the globe, and British trading interests are even more widely distributed. This creates the need for a navy that can move quickly to defend these territories and interests. Meanwhile Britain has been actively involved with the United States and other allies to pursue common interests in areas such as the Middle East.

To pursue these objectives, the Royal Navy today maintains a total fleet of nearly 100 vessels, featuring seven attack submarines, and six destroyers. To staff these and the Royal Navy's aircraft, bases, and fighting forces, a total force of over 35,000 is maintained, led by over 6,600 officers.

In short, while Britannia may no longer rule the waves, it still seeks to have an active say in who does.

THE UNITED STATES NAVY

Today's United States Navy is part of the Defense Department. As the largest government agency in the United States, the Defense Department has a budget bigger than that of most nations. It has in its employ more than 2.1 million persons, including over 700,000 civilians.

ADMINISTRATION

Until 1947, the Navy was a separate branch of the government. The National Security Act of 1947 created the Department of Defense, headed by a civilian cabinet officer, the secretary of defense.

Under the Defense Department the Department of the Navy has three major responsibilities: its administration in Washington, D.C.; its forces at sea; and its land installations. The department is headed by a civilian Secretary of the Navy. This has not been a cabinet position since the reorganization act of 1947. The secretary is assisted

Ray Mabus, who was sworn in as Secretary of the Navy in 2009, administering the oath of office to an ensign of the United States Navy. *U.S. Navy photo by MC 3rd Class Billy Ho*

by one Under Secretary of the Navy and four assistant secretaries, each of whom has specific responsibilities. One is in charge of financial management; another, of manpower and reserves; the third, of research, development, and acquisitions; and the fourth, of installations and environment.

The top military officer of the Navy is the chief of naval operations, or CNO—always a senior admiral. It is the CNO's job to put into effect policies made by the civilian directors of the department. As a member of the Joint Chiefs of Staff, the CNO is the president's chief adviser on naval affairs and is not outranked by any officer unless another naval officer sits as chairman of the Joint Chiefs. The CNO is in direct command of the Navy's operating forces and is assisted by deputy CNOs in charge of manpower and training, submarine warfare, surface warfare, logistics, air warfare, and plans and operations. Also administered by the Department of the Navy is the United States Marine Corps, the nation's principal amphibious arm. Like the CNO, the commandant of the Marine Corps reports to the Secretary of the Navy. Other commands within the department include those overseeing the following: manpower, personnel, education, and training; integration of capabilities and resources; communications networks; the medical arm of the Navy; reserves; material readiness and logistics; information plans and strategy; and test and evaluation and technology requirements.

FORCES AT SEA

In the 2010s, the Navy's forces were distributed among six numbered fleets around the world: the Third, the Fourth, the Fifth, the Sixth, the Seventh, and the Tenth. Missing numbers in the sequence typically represent fleets that are no longer active.

The Third and Seventh Fleets operate in the Pacific Ocean, with the Third Fleet concentrating on defense of the West Coast of the United States and the Seventh Fleet focusing on the Pacific Rim of Asia.

The Fourth Fleet covers the Caribbean Sea, the Gulf of Mexico, South America, and Central America. The Fifth Fleet patrols a wide area including the eastern Mediterranean Sea, the Persian Gulf, and the Red Sea. The Sixth Fleet operates primarily in the Mediterranean and Western Atlantic. Finally, the Tenth Fleet operates out of Fort Meade, Md., with a focus on cyber operations.

In time of war or national emergency, additional ships are drawn from a reserve, and the Coast Guard is also assigned to the Navy. In normal times the Coast Guard is part of the Department of Homeland Security.

When in action, fleets are deployed in two basic formations: carrier strike groups, which are based around aircraft carriers, and expeditionary strike groups, which are based around amphibious assault ships. These formations may be further divided into smaller groupings designed to do specific jobs.

These smaller groupings may be formed for tasks such as combatting enemy submarines or making amphibious landings. An antisubmarine force may include an aircraft carrier laden with specially equipped airplanes and helicopters, a group of destroyers, and submarines of its own. An amphibious striking force is assembled to seize enemy-held islands or coasts. The ingeniously designed ships of such a unit can transport Marines or Army troops across the ocean and land them and their equipment on an open beach; or they can deposit them behind the enemy by using helicopters. Other ships and airplanes support the landing with gunfire, bombs, and missiles.

Logistic support forces enable task forces to remain at sea, far from their bases, for long periods. Their various ships carry fuel, ammunition, food, and other supplies and can transfer their cargoes to the fighting ships while both are in motion.

SHORE UNITS AND ACTIVITIES

To support its forces at sea, the Navy maintains about 90 major shore and field installations. These include naval district headquarters, air facilities and stations, reserve training units, communications stations, fleet intelligence centers, hospitals, laboratories, medical centers, shipyards, and supply centers. Many of these are located along coasts, where they can most directly serve the forces at sea.

For purposes of administration the United States and its overseas territories have been divided into nine naval districts. Each district is headed by a combatant commander, who supervises and coordinates the naval activities within the district.

NAVAL RESERVES

In time of war or national emergency, the Navy's reserves may be called into service. Members of the Naval Reserve hold civilian jobs, but they attend weekly training

Rear Admiral Gretchen Herbert, commander of the Navy Cyber Forces, observing a demonstration. Opportunities for women in the Navy have expanded greatly, with more women serving in positions once only open to men. *U.S. Navy photo by MC 1st Class Joshua J. Wah*

sessions and serve on active duty for two weeks each year. A great many ships are also held in reserve.

Women have served in the United States Navy since 1942. At that time they were members of the WAVES—Women Accepted for Voluntary Emergency Service. Women have been allowed to be members of the regular Navy for decades, though for many years their roles were limited. After the Pentagon announced that it was lifting its ban on women in combat in early 2013, roles for women in the Navy were projected to expand even more.

SEABEES

The best-known logistical sections of the Navy during World War II were the Construction Battalions, a name popularly shortened to CBs, or Seabees. These were men who could both fight and do construction work in combat zones. The Seabees build roads and airfields, machine shops, barracks, power plants, fortifications, communications systems, and supply depots. In World War II, many of these men had been construction workers in civilian life.

Within the Seabees are special units for amphibious operations and antiguerrilla campaigns. The underwater demolition teams, or frogmen, clear underwater obstacles from beaches where amphibious landings are to be made. There are also special units of frogmen called sea, air, and land teams, or SEALs. Trained in underwater demolition,

NAVY SEALS

A SEAL (in full, Sea, Air, and Land) in the United States Navy is a member of a special operations force trained to engage in direct raids or assaults on enemy targets, conduct reconnaissance missions to report on enemy activity (especially prior to beach landings), and take part in action against terrorist groups.

The SEALs trace their heritage to various elite units in World War II, particularly to naval combat

Navy SEALs in Fallujah, Iraq, waiting for a night mission involving the capture of Iraqi insurgent leaders. *John Moore/ Getty Images*

demolition units (NCDUs) and underwater demolition teams (UDTs) whose "frogmen" were trained to destroy obstacles on enemy-held beaches prior to amphibious landings in Europe and the Pacific.

In 1961, Pres. John F. Kennedy called for an increase in special forces of all kinds to be specifically trained for the conduct of unconventional warfare. In response, the following year the Navy created the first two SEAL teams with personnel taken from existing UDTs.

SEAL units took part in several U.S. military engagements abroad, including the Vietnam War, protection of merchant shipping in the Persian Gulf in 1987–88 during the Iran-Iraq War, the intervention in Panama in 1989, and the liberation of Kuwait during the Persian Gulf War (1990–91). During the global war on terrorism following the September 11 attacks of 2001, SEAL teams were in almost constant rotation, particularly in the Afghanistan War (from 2001) and the Iraq War (from 2003). In these conflicts they conducted numerous counterguerrilla and counterterrorist operations, often far from the coastal or riverine environments with which they are usually associated—the most prominent operation being the killing in 2011 of al-Qaeda leader Osama bin Laden in northern Pakistan.

these men can also operate from submarines or on land by parachute drop in enemy coastal areas.

THE NAVY IN EXPLORATION

Since the seas are its battlefield, the Navy has an intense interest in exploration of the ocean. Navy oceanographers chart great stretches of ocean floor that have never before been mapped. Others study underwater sound transmission. Both efforts are vital for submarine operations.

The Navy is also involved in a wide variety of scientific research. Its microbiologists study ways of preventing the spread of infectious diseases, both for the benefit of naval personnel and to bring humanitarian aid to people in other countries. Biochemists are involved in researching ways to harness sustainable energy from sources such as the sun and the oceans. Navy meteorologists study ways to better forecast weather patterns and events. Other Navy scientists are working on the prototype for a new atomic clock.

The Navy has a number of ships and underwater craft for exploration and research.

The most unusual is probably the Floating Instrument Platform, or FLIP. Unpowered, it floats on the surface while being towed into position. Then its stern is flooded, and it stands on end in the sea with only a few feet of its bow above water. The 355-foot (108-m) ship is used in studies of waves, marine life, and underwater sound.

Exploration of the Arctic and Antarctic regions is a longstanding naval interest. Admiral Richard E. Byrd was the first man to fly over both poles. In Antarctica, the Navy maintains a number of year-round

The Navy's Floating Instrument Platform (FLIP) standing on its end in the Pacific Ocean. *U.S. Navy photo by John F. Williams*

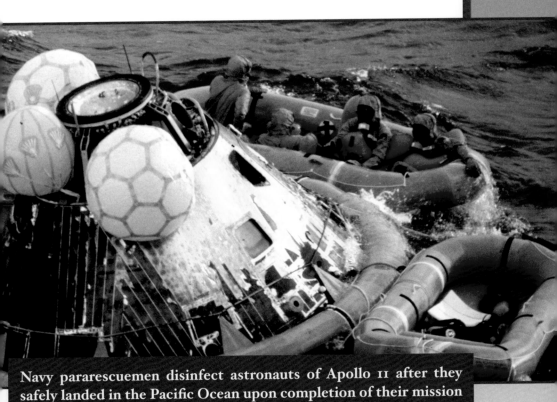

Navy pararescuemen disinfect astronauts of Apollo 11 after they safely landed in the Pacific Ocean upon completion of their mission in 1969. *8383/Gamma-Rapho/Getty Images*

stations for weather research and other scientific studies. At the opposite end of Earth, nuclear-powered submarines have passed from the Atlantic to the Pacific beneath the polar ice cap. To study the Arctic seas, Navy and university scientists spend winters on floating ice islands—blocks of ice about 2 to 3 miles (3 to 5 km) on a side and perhaps 50 feet (15 m) thick.

The Navy has also played a role in space exploration. Ships provide satellite- and missile-tracking facilities, and they recovered astronauts who landed in the sea after orbital flights. In May 1961, Navy Cmdr. Alan B. Shepard was the first American in space, and the first person to set foot on the moon was Neil Armstrong, who had been a Navy pilot in the Korean War. All the first crew of Skylab, the first orbiting space laboratory, were Navy aviators. A four-satellite navigational system was put into operation in 1964, and other Navy satellites have been launched since.

HISTORY OF THE UNITED STATES NAVY

American naval history began with the Revolutionary War. On Oct. 13, 1775, the Continental Congress appointed Silas Deane, John Adams, and John Langdon to fit two warships. Eventually more than a dozen ships were commissioned for the new Navy. They fought under such commanders as John Paul Jones, John Barry, and Esek Hopkins. On Dec. 22, 1775, Hopkins was named commodore of the Navy. He led the first American fleet to sea on Feb. 17, 1776. It sank or captured 200 British warcraft and 800 other ships. A French victory over a British fleet off Chesapeake Bay on Sept. 5, 1781, hastened the end of the war and helped assure George Washington's victory at Yorktown. After the war the Continental Navy was disbanded.

POST-REVOLUTIONARY PERIOD

No American naval force existed until March 27, 1794, when Congress authorized

THE FIRST SUBMARINE ATTACKS

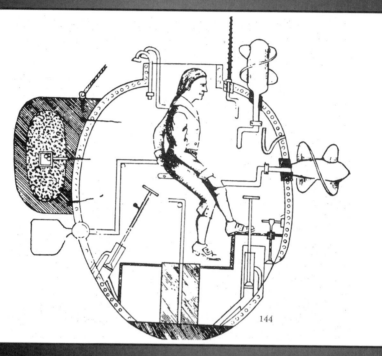

144

An illustration of the interior of the *Turtle*. *MPI/Archive Photos/Getty Images*

The first submergible used for military purposes was David Bushnell's *Turtle*, a one-man, wooden, barrel-like craft employed during the American Revolution against British warships. Powered by hand-turned propellers, the vessel was designed to approach anchored ships while it was at least partially submerged and to attach an explosive charge to the target's hull with an external screwlike device. Although the craft itself worked well enough, the armament device proved unsuccessful.

the building of six frigates: the *United States*, *Constitution*, *President*, *Chesapeake*, *Constellation*, and *Congress*. On April 30, 1798, the Navy Department was established with Benjamin Stoddert as the first secretary.

Dubbed "Old Ironsides" after its victory over the British frigate *Guerrière* in the War of 1812, the *Constitution* was rebuilt after 1830 and remained in service for 48 more years. The rebuilding was prompted by a public outcry inspired by Oliver Wendell Holmes's poem "Old Ironsides," which he wrote on hearing that the famous ship had been ordered destroyed. Today, the ship may be viewed at the Boston Navy Yard.

The new American ships performed well in 1799–1800 during the "undeclared war with France." In 1803–04, they defeated the land and sea forces of the Barbary pirates of North Africa. During the War of 1812, the United States had only 17 warships to face a British fleet of at least 600. Yet the American frigates did surprisingly well. Designed by Joshua Humphreys, the frigates had thicker sides and heavier guns, and they excelled in speed and maneuverability. By December 1812, the Royal Navy was under orders not to take on these frigates with less than squadron strength.

Apart from suppressing piracy in North Africa and engagements in the Mexican War, the Navy had no serious conflicts until the Civil War. There were, nevertheless, some significant milestones. In 1821, the *Congress* became the first American warship to visit China. The *Vincennes* was the first Navy ship to go around the world (1826–30). The United States Naval Observatory was established in 1830. A naval expedition under Charles Wilkes went around the world in 1838–42, exploring Antarctica and the Pacific. The *Michigan* was commissioned as the first iron-hulled ship in 1843. In 1845, the Naval Academy was established in Annapolis, Md. In 1846, the *Columbus* visited Japan, and eight years later Commodore Matthew Perry signed a treaty with Japan, opening that country to American trade.

THE CIVIL WAR

The best-known naval incident during the Civil War was the indecisive battle between the *Monitor* and the *Merrimack* in March 1862. Other naval activities included blockading Confederate ports and gunboat actions along the Mississippi and other western rivers.

BATTLE OF THE *MONITOR* AND *MERRIMACK*

On the afternoon of March 8, 1862, five vessels of the United States Navy lay at anchor in Hampton Roads, Va. Suddenly a strange-looking object moved through the water toward the United States vessel *Cumberland* from the Confederate stronghold in Norfolk, Va. It was a reconstructed United States ship, the *Merrimack* (renamed the *Virginia*). The vessel had been sunk when the Norfolk navy yard was abandoned at the beginning of the war. The Confederates had raised the vessel, cut off the sides, and covered what was left with iron plates. This was one of the earliest practical applications of armor to a warship.

The ironclad steered straight for the *Cumberland*. It was met by heavy fire, but, when it reached the *Cumberland*, its iron beak cut through the side of the wooden vessel "as a knife goes through cheese." The *Merrimack* next set fire to the *Congress* with red-hot shot from its guns. Then the vessel steamed away to prepare for its next victory.

By the next morning, however, the situation was entirely changed. When the *Merrimack* started toward the *Minnesota*, preparing to dispose of it as quickly as the two victims of the previous day, there suddenly appeared in the ironclad's path an odd object, about one-fourth the *Merrimack's* size and resembling a "cheese-box on a raft." This was the famous *Monitor*, a Union ironclad designed by John Ericsson, a Swedish engineer.

The fight between the two ships began at once and lasted for nearly four hours. The *Monitor* was

The Battle of the *Monitor* and the *Merrimack*, also called the Battle of Hampton Roads, the first battle between ironclads. *Buyenlarge/Archive Photos/Getty Images*

more easily handled than the *Merrimack*, but its shots could not do much harm to the other's iron sides. On the other hand, the *Monitor's* single revolving turret offered a hopeless target for its opponent. Thousands of people stood on the shore and breathlessly watched the combat. The distance between the vessels varied from half a mile to a few yards. The *Monitor's* commander was wounded, and the *Merrimack*, badly damaged, steamed back to Norfolk.

This fight between the *Merrimack* and *Monitor* was one of the most important naval battles ever fought, for it made the warships of all the old navies useless. All countries had to discard their wooden vessels and to begin building ironclads. During the Civil War, the Union was able to build more iron ships faster than the Confederacy could.

Actions were also fought against Confederate commerce raiders on the high seas.

POST–CIVIL WAR PERIOD

After the Civil War, the Navy stagnated for nearly 20 years. In 1883, Congress authorized the building of a modern navy, and the Naval War College was founded in 1884. The new fleet proved itself in the Spanish-American War with victories in the Philippines and Cuba.

After the war, construction was begun on a stronger battle fleet—largely at the insistence of Theodore Roosevelt, who became president in 1901. It was during Roosevelt's term of office that the first great modern naval battle took place—the Battle of Tsushima (May 1905) between Japan and Russia in the Russo-Japanese War. To impress the world with American naval power, Roosevelt sent a fleet on an around-the-world tour from 1907 to 1908. Part of his purpose was to convince the Japanese that the United States had vital interests in the western Pacific.

THE WORLD WARS AND COLD WAR

World War I promoted a further buildup of the Navy, and the onset of World War II provided even greater incentive. By the end of World War II, the United States Navy was the largest and most powerful in the world.

With the onset of the Cold War, the

BATTLE OF MIDWAY

In June of 1942, a strong invasion force of Japanese moved directly against the Hawaiian Islands. American ships, Navy planes, and Army planes from Midway Island fought a four-day battle against the invaders. The Americans lost a carrier, a destroyer, and 150 planes. The invaders, however, were completely defeated. They lost four aircraft carriers, two heavy cruisers, three destroyers, and 330 planes. Meanwhile a Japanese force occupied several of the Aleutian Islands.

The Battle of Midway ended serious Japanese expansion and is considered the turning point in the Pacific. Coming less than seven months after the Japanese attack on Pearl Harbor, the battle turned the tide against Japan and pointed the way to an American victory in the Pacific three years later.

CHESTER NIMITZ

Chester Nimitz was commander of the U.S. Pacific Fleet during World War II. One of the Navy's foremost administrators and strategists, he commanded all land and sea forces in the central Pacific area.

A graduate (1905) of the U.S. Naval Academy at Annapolis, Nimitz served in World War I as chief of

Fleet Admiral Chester Nimitz signing documents of surrender from Japan in 1945 on board the USS *Missouri*. *Hulton Archive/Getty Images*

staff to the commander of the U.S. Atlantic submarine force, a tour of duty that convinced him of the effectiveness of submarine warfare. He held a variety of posts at sea and on shore until 1939, when he was appointed chief of the Bureau of Navigation of the United States Navy.

After the Japanese attack on Pearl Harbor (December 1941), Nimitz was elevated to commander in chief of the Pacific Fleet, a command that brought both land and sea forces under his authority. By June 1942, he had proudly announced the decisive victory at the Battle of Midway and the Coral Sea, where enemy losses were 10 times greater than those of the United States at Pearl Harbor. In succeeding years, the historic battles of the Solomon Islands (1942–43), the Gilbert Islands (1943), the Marshalls, Marianas, Palaus, and Philippines (1944), and Iwo Jima and Okinawa (1945) were fought under his direction.

The Japanese capitulation was signed aboard his flagship, the USS *Missouri*, in Tokyo Bay on Sept. 2, 1945. In December 1944, Nimitz had been promoted to the Navy's newest and highest rank—that of fleet admiral.

After the war, Nimitz served as chief of naval operations (1945–47). In 1947, in answer to interrogatories by the German Adm. Karl Dönitz, on trial for war crimes, Nimitz gave his justification for the unrestricted nature of U.S. submarine warfare in the Pacific during World War II. With E.B. Potter he edited *Sea Power, a Naval History* (1960).

Soviet Union overtook the United States in many aspects of naval power. After the collapse of the Soviet Union in 1991, the former Soviet Navy was placed under the joint control of the members of the Commonwealth of Independent States. This arrangement was disputed by Ukraine, which claimed parts of the Navy, especially the strategic Black Sea fleet, as its own.

NAVAL ENGAGEMENTS IN THE LATE 20TH AND EARLY 21ST CENTURIES

With the end of the Cold War, military priorities for the United States shifted from preparing for a major confrontation with another superpower to preparing to fight a series of smaller engagements throughout the world. The United States Navy has had to adapt accordingly.

In 1991, the United States Navy participated with a multinational force in the liberation of Kuwait, which had been invaded by Iraq. The Navy was able to array over 130 warships in the region, including six aircraft carriers. Although Iraq's negligible naval capability limited the conflict at sea, the ability of the U.S. to launch carrier-based strikes into Iraq was instrumental in winning a quick victory.

Providing a basis for air operations was also a major part of the Navy's role in U.S. invasions of Afghanistan and Iraq in the early 21st century. In between the first Gulf War and those later conflicts, the Navy had also supported much more limited U.S. interventions in Haiti, Somalia, Bosnia, and Kosovo.

The most celebrated naval action of the

Pres. Barack Obama announcing the death of terrorist Osama bin Laden in 2011. The Navy's SEAL Team 6 found and killed him in Abbottabad, Pakistan. *Getty Images*

early 21st century occurred hundreds of miles away from the nearest sea. In 2011, the Navy's SEAL Team 6 located and killed notorious terrorist Osama bin Laden in northeastern Pakistan. Previously, Navy SEALs (known formally as the Naval Special Warfare Development Group) had participated in missions including the rescue of Grenada's governor-general during the 1983 revolution on that island, and the capture of former Panamanian dictator Manuel Noriega, who was wanted in the United States on drug-related charges.

That SEAL Team 6 should be capable of such diverse missions so far away from the open seas shows just how versatile the modern United States Navy has become. This versatility is a necessity given the unpredictable, variable, and often highly localized nature of modern warfare. This has changed the way Navy personnel are trained and has affected the ships and equipment they use.

Although it is impossible to predict exactly what changes lie ahead for the Navy, two major evolutions in personnel policies are sure to expand the pool of talent available to serve in the military. With the ending of the "Don't Ask, Don't Tell" standard in 2011, gays were permitted to serve openly in the U.S. Armed Forces, and in early 2013 another change in Pentagon policy opened the door for women to serve directly in combat roles. These policy shifts could give the United States Navy more resources to draw from as it faces the challenges that the remainder of the 21st century will bring.

CONCLUSION

It is easy to look at the weaponry carried by modern navies and focus just on the destructive power of these fighting forces. However, it is also important to remember that these same navies help keep the peace through their presence around the globe, conduct research that can benefit all of mankind, and are often used to deliver humanitarian relief to troubled areas.

Changes in personnel policies in the 21st century are a reminder that as much as navies might be defined by their ships and other equipment, they are ultimately human organizations. Even as technology and tactics have redefined modern navies, it is that human element that carries naval tradition forward from the past to the future.

GLOSSARY

amphibious Relating to or adapted for both land and water; also, executed by coordinated action of land, sea, and air forces organized for invasion.

ballistic missile A missile that moves under its own power, is guided as it rises in a steeply curving path, and falls freely on the way back to earth.

battleship A capital ship of the world's navies from about 1860, when it began to supplant the wooden-hulled, sail-driven ship of the line, to World War II, when its preeminent position was taken over by the aircraft carrier.

broadside The side of a ship above the waterline; all the guns on one side of a ship, also, their simultaneous discharge.

caravel A light sailing ship of the 15th, 16th, and 17th centuries in Europe, much-used by the Spanish and Portuguese for long voyages.

carrack A sailing ship of the 14th–17th centuries that was usually built with three masts, the mainmast and foremast being rigged with square sails and the mizzenmast rigged with a fore-and-aft triangular lateen sail.

convoy Vessels sailing under the protection of an armed escort.

cruiser A large surface warship built for high speed and great cruising radius, capable of not only defending its own fleet and coastlines but also threatening those of the enemy.

destroyer A fast naval vessel that has served a variety of functions since the late 19th century, mainly in defense of surface fleets and convoys.

force projection A country's ability to conduct military operations outside of its own borders.

forecastle The forward part of the upper deck of a ship.

frigate A square-rigged war vessel intermediate between a corvette and a ship of the line; also, a modern warship that is smaller than a destroyer.

galleon A full-rigged sailing ship that was built primarily for war, and which developed in the 15th and 16th centuries.

galley A short crescent-shaped seagoing ship of classical antiquity propelled chiefly by oars though generally having a mast carrying an oblong sail.

gangplank A movable bridge used in boarding or leaving a ship at a pier.

grappling hook A hook usually with multiple prongs that is typically attached to a rope and is used for grabbing, grappling, or gripping.

grappling iron A hooked iron for anchoring a boat, grappling ships to each other, or recovering sunken objects.

liburnian A fast light large-sailed sharp-prowed galley invented by the Liburnian pirates.

man-of-war A combatant warship of a recognized navy.

melee A naval battle in which ships break formation and engage an enemy ship at close range.

payload The load carried by a vehicle exclusive of what is necessary for its operation.

proximity fuse A fuse for a projectile that uses the principle of radar to detect the presence of a target within the projectile's effective range.

ship of the line A ship superior to a frigate and usually a 74-gun or 3-decker ship.

ship-of-the-line warfare A columnar naval-battle formation developed by the British and Dutch in the mid-17th century whereby each ship followed in the wake of the ship ahead of it, which maximized the new firing power of the broadside and marked a final break with the tactics of galley warfare.

FOR MORE INFORMATION

Canadian War Museum
1 Vimy Place
Ottawa, ON KIA OM8
Canada
(800) 555-5621
Web site: http://www.warmuseum.ca
Through exhibitions featuring art, artifacts, and memoirs, as well as interactive presentations, the Canadian War Museum engages visitors with the history of the Canadian military from its inception to the present. It also offers a variety of educational programs on the history of the Canadian armed forces.

China Lake Museum Foundation
P.O. Box 217
Ridgecrest, CA 93556
(760) 939-3530
Web site: http://www.chinalakemuseum.org
Also known as the U.S. Naval Museum of

Armament & Technology, the China Lake Museum began as a testing and research facility used by the California Institute of Technology for rocket development during World War II. Today, the China Lake Museum educates the public through its tours and exhibits, which boast some of the most important arms and technology in the history of the United States Navy.

Directorate of History and Heritage (DHH)
National Defence Headquarters
101 Colonel By Drive
Ottawa, ON KIA OK2
Canada
(613) 998-7058
Web site: http://www.cmp-cpm.forces.gc.ca
The DHH is an organization under the Canadian Department of National Defence dating back to the First World War. Its museum system and publications offer a wealth of information on the history of the Canadian forces for researchers and the general public.

National Museum of the U.S. Navy
805 Kidder Breese Street SE
Washington Navy Yard, DC 20374
(202) 433-4882

Web site: http://www.history.navy.mil
The National Museum of the U.S. Navy hosts a collection of some of the most important naval artifacts in the history of the United States Navy. It chronicles the Navy's history from its inception to the present to inform, educate, and inspire both naval personnel and the general public. It also hosts an on-site library, archives, and photographic and other research facilities.

Naval Historical Foundation (NHF)
1306 Dahlgren Avenue SE
Washington Navy Yard, DC 20374
(888) 880-0102
Web site: http://www.navyhistory.org
The NHF works to promote and teach the history of the United States Navy, hosting large archives of important naval manuscripts and other historical documents, as well as an on-site museum with exhibits on naval history. Its STEM Teacher Fellowship program trains teachers from around the United States on integrating STEM-focused educational lesson plans into their classrooms.

Navy League of the United States (NLUS)
2300 Wilson Boulevard, Suite 200
Arlington, VA 22201
(800) 356-5760
Web site: http://www.navyleague.org
The NLUS was founded in 1902 to provide a voice to civilians supporting the United States Navy, Marine Corps, and Coast Guard. It seeks to develop the morale of armed forces personnel, promotes education and awareness of the Sea Services of the U.S. Armed Forces, and encourages youth involvement through its Naval Sea Cadets Corps, Junior R.O.T.C., and Young Marines programs.

WEB SITES

Due to the changing nature of Internet links, Rosen Educational Services has developed an online list of Web sites related to the subject of this book. This site is updated regularly. Please use this link to access the list:

http://www.rosenlinks.com/armed/navy

FOR FURTHER READING

Besel, Jennifer M. *The U.S. Navy SEALs: The Missions*. North Mankato, MN: Capstone, 2013.

Bow, James. *Navy SEALs*. New York, NY: Crabtree, 2012.

Dolan, Edward F. *Careers in the U.S. Navy*. New York, NY: Benchmark Books, 2009.

Grove, Mark J., Philip D. Grove, and Alastair Finlan. *World War II: The War at Sea*. New York, NY: Rosen, 2010.

Jackson, Robert. *101 Great Warships*. New York, NY: Rosen, 2010.

Jackson, Robert. *Warships: Inside & Out*. New York, NY : Rosen, 2011.

Montana, Jack. *Navy SEALs*. Broomall, PA: Mason Crest, 2010.

Nardo, Don. *Special Operations: Amphibious Warfare*. Greensboro, NC: Morgan Reynolds, 2012.

Orr, Tamra. *Your Career in the Navy*. New York, NY: Rosen, 2011.

Varble, Derek. *The Suez Crisis*. New York, NY: Rosen, 2008.

Walker, Sally M. *Secrets of a Civil War Submarine: Solving the Mysteries of the H.L. Hunley*. Minneapolis, MN: Lerner Publishing Group, 2005.

INDEX